Brockhampton Church

Brockhampton Church

An Experiment in Arts and Crafts Architecture

Innox Hill Publications

2016

IN MEMORY OF

Matthew Hyde

FIRST PUBLISHED 2016

© Graham Burgess 2016

ISBN 978 15411668 9 9

Text and cover design © Lyn Davies
lyndaviesdesign.com

Contents

*Architecture is the easy
and expressive handling of materials
in masterly experimental building
– it is the craftsmen's drama*

W.R LETHABY
The Builder's Art & The Craftsman
1892

Introduction

All Saints Church, Brockhampton, Herefordshire was built in 1901–2 by W.R.Lethaby in the Arts and Crafts tradition. It has long been acclaimed – not least by Nikolaus Pevsner who though it 'one of the most convincing and most impressive churches of its date in any country'[1] and, more recently, by Simon Jenkins who wrote that it is 'an expression of past time, yet without imitation or pastiche'[2], and proclaimed by Peter Davey as 'one of the greatest monuments to the Arts and Crafts Movement'[3]. This study seeks to explore what lies behind the building's acknowledged qualities.

The Arts and Crafts Movement

The heyday of the design phenomenon which became known as the Arts & Crafts Movement ran from about 1890 until the First World War. It encompassed activities as diverse as typography and blacksmithing, garden design and furniture-making. It also included architecture. Although examples of Arts & Crafts work can, with a little familiarity, be readily identified as such, it is distinguished more as a manifestation of an underlying philosophy than necessarily by its style alone. The range of styles was wide and practitioners were widespread and prolific. Consequently, the Movement has left a considerable legacy in Britain as well as spawning offspring in Scandinavia, Germany and the USA. It is testament to its quality and enduring appeal that much of this survives today.

Despite the irony of its creation of artefacts and buildings for wealthy clients, the Arts & Crafts movement's roots were firmly in socialist philosophy. This was not the remote theoretical socialism of Marx and Engels, but the somewhat more accessible and pragmatic socialism of activists and writers such as William Morris and John Ruskin. It was based (as originally had been Marx's ideas), on the notion of the fundamental human need for meaningful work. According to this, human beings are at their most fulfilled when they are engaged in making things. This is only true, however, so long as they are able to make things according to their own free will. Coercion or compulsion takes away the pleasure and meaning of the creative act and ultimately crushes this basic source of human fulfilment leaving the individual diminished, dependent and alienated. The industrial revolution had created many marvels, but the millions of alienated factory workers surviving in polluted and squalid slums was not one of them. For Marx the solution had been the 'dictatorship of the proletariat' followed by (an undefined) future communist society. For Morris it was exploring ways in which people might reclaim fulfilment in creative work in their own lives through a revival of traditional crafts, many of which were being rapidly lost to industrialisation. Morris's own life was exemplary in this respect. He turned his hand to an extremely wide range of crafts, even re-creating some, notably tapestry-making, which had long since died out in Britain.

Beyond this, Arts and Crafts design and manufacture was about high-quality and usually locally-sourced materials. It was about relevance to context, whether historical, cultural or geological, and it was about human-scale and simple human delight.

Figure 1. Drawing of William Lethaby by Sir William Rothenstein, 1921.

The Architect

W.R. LETHABY

Of all the architects and craftsmen of the Arts and Crafts tradition in the generation which followed that of Ruskin and Morris, few were to be as influential as W.R.Lethaby. Having worked for Norman Shaw for ten years, Lethaby set up his own practice in 1889 and soon found himself one of the instigators of a new movement based on the ideas of those earlier thinkers. Indeed, although he wrote many books and articles throughout his life including *Architecture Mysticism & Myth*, his well-known pioneering work on architectural symbolism, it was primarily as an energetic interpreter of existing ideas which marks him out, particularly in his educational principles and built work.

In 1893 he was elected to the committee of SPAB (Society for the Protection of Ancient Buildings), and in 1894 was appointed Art Inspector to the Technical Education Board, London (his application being supported by, among others, Norman Shaw, Edward Burne-Jones, Philip Webb, Walter Crane, and William Morris). In 1896 he had been instrumental in establishing the Central School of Arts and Crafts to which he was appointed joint director (and *de facto* principal, a position which was formalised in 1902, following completion of Brockhampton Church).

The contemporary emphasis within established artistic and architectural education was on drawing skills and on copying historic styles. Lethaby and his peers thought this approach futile and not conducive to good practical, or beautiful, design. As Godfrey Rubens summarised

> The lesson taught by the Arts and Crafts movement – so his argument ran – was that the only true style, a style with vital beauty, must be the result of experiments with material made by [someone] who was both its designer and maker.[4]

Throughout his fourteen years at the Central School Lethaby championed a hands-on approach to art and architecture, believing that architectural and artistic skills must grow out of a sound knowledge of materials, techniques and structures. To this end, the teachers appointed by Lethaby were exclusively master craftsmen who taught part-time but made their primary living from their art. The Central School was so successful that it had soon twice moved into larger accommodation, eventually coming under the auspices of the Local Authority in 1908. The school's list of alumni provides a who's who of British design extending well into the 20th century.

In this study I aim to show how Lethaby experimented with the principles which he was espousing at the Central School, using the opportunity of a commission he had been given to design and build a new church at Brockhampton in Herefordshire.

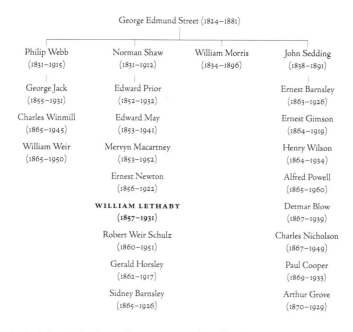

George Edmund Street (1824–1881)

Philip Webb (1831–1915)	Norman Shaw (1831–1912)	William Morris (1834–1896)	John Sedding (1838–1891)
George Jack (1855–1931)	Edward Prior (1852–1932)		Ernest Barnsley (1863–1926)
Charles Winmill (1865–1945)	Edward May (1853–1941)		Ernest Gimson (1864–1919)
William Weir (1865–1950)	Mervyn Macartney (1853–1952)		Henry Wilson (1864–1934)
	Ernest Newton (1856–1922)		Alfred Powell (1865–1960)
	WILLIAM LETHABY (1857–1931)		Detmar Blow (1867–1939)
	Robert Weir Schulz (1860–1951)		Charles Nicholson (1867–1949)
	Gerald Horsley (1862–1917)		Paul Cooper (1869–1933)
	Sidney Barnsley (1865–1926)		Arthur Grove (1870–1929)

Lethaby's place in the pantheon of Arts and Crafts architects can be seen in this 'tree' of architectural offices.

Lethaby's Architectural Philosophy

By 1895 Lethaby was advising the London County Council's Technical Education Board on appropriate training for students of architecture. His main argument – that 'professional' architects producing designs for others to build would be 'an enemy of good building' was taken directly from Ruskin's essay 'The Nature of Gothic'[5]. His suggested core reading for architectural students consisted of

> 'an accessible version of [Pugin's] main line of thought, Ruskin's *The Seven Lamps of Architecture* and *The Stones of Venice*, especially the chapter 'The Nature of Gothic'; Morris's essays 'Hopes and Fears for Art' and 'Gothic Architecture'; Viollet-le-Duc's article on Gothic Construction [in his *Rational Architecture*] and finally Choisy's work on Roman and Byzantine building'[6]

It is hardly surprising, then, that Lethaby's church at Brockhampton, built so soon after these recommendations, should have sought to exemplify many of the principles contained within this reading list. Moreover, Lethaby had been recently stung by criticism of his approach to the building of Avon Tyrrell (1892) – a large country house in the New Forest, near Christchurch – by the Scottish Arts and Crafts architect Robert Lorrimer who had written

> What does the man preach? That modern work fails because it is all done in the office and isn't worked out on the spot as in the old days as afore time! Well if you'd been with me (I wish to God you had been) we'd have agreed a dozen things that failed in this very particular...[7]

There had been 229 detailed drawings for Avon Tyrrell and a main contractor. For Brockhampton Church, by contrast, there were reputed to have been only eleven, and work proceeded by direct labour under the personal supervision of Lethaby himself. Even these few drawings were fairly sketchy[8]. Indeed, the church itself can be seen as a veritable realisation in working practices, not to mention in concrete and stone, of the principles found in the works of the writers cited above as well as in Lethaby's own written works. These principles may be broadly summarised as follows:

1. *A.W.N. Pugin (1812–1852)*. The importance of honesty of construction, of decoration consisting in the emphasis of structural necessities and of forms being true to the nature of the material of which they are constructed, can be said to have originated, as an architectural theory of the nineteenth century, in the mind of Pugin. Lethaby's statement, that the only two purposes of a building were 'service and delight'[9], can also be seen to have its roots in Pugin's ideas.

2. *John Ruskin (1819–1900)*. Certainly would have read Pugin, but, possibly because of Pugin's Catholicism, chose not to acknowledge his debt. The themes of honesty of construction persist in Ruskin's prolific output, as does the appropriateness of architecture to cultural and climatic context. In addition, Ruskin highlighted a concern for the spiritual well-being of the workman who, during the expanding industrialisation of the times, was seen to be increasingly alienated from the fundamental human fulfilment to be found in meaningful work. Ruskin also placed great emphasis on the resulting vitality of such work made evident within the construction of the building itself.

3. *William Morris (1834–1896)*. The primary interests of Morris were in the quest for meaningful work in all aspects of manufacture, much of which he took from Ruskin. His enthusiasm for Ruskin's writing, however, was largely limited to those works concerned with architecture, particularly *The seven Lamps of Architecture*, and *The Stones of Venice*. The production of any manufactured thing ought, according to Morris, to be essentially 'art' insofar as any work which could not be enjoyed was, to his mind, not worth doing. He became a committed socialist and was exemplary in terms of being a theorist who also engaged fully in the practicalities of creativity.

4. *Eugene Viollet-le-Duc (1814–1879)*. This French architect was also inspired by reading Ruskin. He went on to study mediaeval buildings in great detail, as had Pugin and Ruskin before him. He

was a prolific writer, architect and restorer of mediaeval buildings. He was also a theorist on architectural education whose ideas chimed closely with Lethaby's, and was an advocate in the use of novel building materials.

5. *Auguste Choisy (1841–1909)*. Another French writer cited by Lethaby, whose work regarding Roman and Byzantine architecture, unfortunately, does not currently appear to be available in English translation.

Of these five writers cited by Lethaby as being key to architectural study, Ruskin overwhelms the others in terms of prominence and influence on the Arts and Crafts movement generally, and on Lethaby in particular. A more detailed analysis of his relevant works will, therefore, be necessary to our understanding Lethaby's own work at Brockhampton.

Pevsner writes that '[Lethaby] gave [Brockhampton] church a mediaeval character without anywhere imitating the past'[10]. The readiest means of understanding how this might have been achieved is to turn to Ruskin's 'The Nature of Gothic' which forms chapter vi in *The Stones of Venice* first published in 1851. In terms of Ruskin's subsequent influence on a new architecture, this was probably his most important piece of writing – indeed, so important had this been to Morris, that *The Nature of Gothic* was among the first publications of Morris's Kelmscott Press in 1891, published as a book in its own right.[11] Lethaby, who in his younger days claimed to have read Ruskin with 'an amused contempt'[12], had since changed his mind. Godfrey Rubens suggests that

> The process may well not have started until in 1888 he read, or possibly. . . re-read that all-important essay 'The Nature of Gothic' from *The Stones of Venice* which Morris considered to be one of the 'very few necessary and inevitable utterances of the century'.[13]

In this essay, or chapter, Ruskin employs a clear structure, suggesting a list, in descending order of importance, of the fundamental criteria for a Gothic building. We must not be too distracted by the term Gothic. Ruskin was, for much of his life, a fierce critic of the 'Gothic Revival'. He believed mediaeval architecture, however, to be organic, capable of many forms, relevant to northern climates and available materials, and the last truly indigenous architecture of Northern Europe. So, although his analysis is ostensibly about discovering the true essential elements of 'Gothic' architecture, there can be little doubt that, for Ruskin, these were intended to be read as desirable properties of all building in northern climates. Indeed, it was read as such my many, if not all, the Arts and Crafts architects.

In his consideration of architectural sculpture, Ruskin suggested that in ancient classical architecture the sculptors and workmen had no room for free expression and were, effectively, slaves[14], *i.e.* they were either highly skilled in executing the exacting designs of others, or else the designs were simplified to the extent to which a regular workman could reproduce them accurately. In mediaeval Christian ornament, on the other hand, the 'individual value of every soul' is recognised and its imperfection dignified in the face of God's greater glory[15]. Thus it was believed by Ruskin and his followers (rightly or wrongly is not important here as it was influential either way) that ordinary mediaeval workmen working on the Gothic cathedrals, were free to 'have a go' at carving corbels, gargoyles and suchlike.

> '... it is, perhaps, the principal admirableness of the Gothic schools of architecture, that they thus receive the results of labour of inferior minds; and out of fragments full of imperfection, and betraying that imperfection at every touch, indulgently raise up a stately and unaccusable whole.'[16]

But it was not, for Ruskin, just a matter of the creation of audacious and vital architecture; it was at least as much about the effect that such freedoms would have had on those engaged in the construction work itself, and how this reflected on the society from which they came. It was, for him, a matter of encouraging true creative work of the sort that came most naturally to human beings. Denying such valuable creativity to one's employees, would be, to this extent, to deny them their humanity. However, this is a difficult transition for workers used to obeying precise instructions. Ask them to think for themselves, so his argument goes, and they will hesitate and make mistakes. Such mistakes must be tolerated, argued Ruskin, because they are evidence of life and humanity and because the building itself will reflect such life and humanity in the errors and inaccuracies evident within it:

> '... they are signs of the life and liberty of every workman who struck the stone; a freedom of thought, and rank in scale of being, such as no laws, no charters, no charities can secure; but which it must be the first aim of all Europe at this day to regain for her children.'[17]

In fact Ruskin had already unearthed numerous examples of significant inaccuracies in mediaeval buildings which appeared to suggest that these were no accidents of workmen struggling with new-found freedoms, but were wilful and deliberate

> '[Such] variations are not merely blunders, nor carelessness, but the result of a fixed scorn, if not dislike, of accuracy in measurements ... variations as subtle as those of Nature.'[18]

(Several convincing examples can be found in chapter v *Stones of Venice* and in chapter v, 'The Lamp of Life' in *The Seven Lamps of Architecture*). This aside, for Ruskin, it was such inaccuracies which gave a building vitality, whatever their origins. If the origins were the setting free of previously 'enslaved' workmen, so much the better. This becomes something of a point of faith – 'No architecture can be truly noble which is not imperfect'[19] and,

> 'The greater and more conspicuous the irregularities, the greater the chances that it is a good [building].'[20]

Furthermore, an important consequence of this general line of thought was an abhorrence of the division of labour into 'Thinkers' (*i.e.* designers) and 'Operatives' who perform the actual manufacture and are generally held to be disdained by the Thinkers. Such divisions were elsewhere called 'alienation' and both Ruskin and Morris sought to dissolve these. For them it could only be through engaging in the physical process of creation that 'thinking' or 'inventing' could be healthy, and, conversely, only through engagement in the design process that an 'operative' or labourer could be made happy in his work through a fuller sense of participation. Believing both of these to be crucial in the creation of a 'great work of art', Ruskin concluded, for example, that 'The architect [should] work in the mason's yard with his men.'[21]

Theory into Practice

Armed with this plethora of ideas and principles, and backed up by his overriding principle of the critical importance of experimentation in creative work, Lethaby was somehow bound to try these out on a dream-project such as the building of a small church. So began the experiment.

Direct Labour

We know that Lethaby chose to take on the role of Master Builder for this project, opted to live much of the time on site, and to order materials and directly employ craftsmen himself. He had not worked in this way before and the experience was not an altogether happy one. Leaving Randall Wells, his keen young architect-builder assistant, in charge during his absences he heard at one point *from his clients* that an arch had collapsed and had to find out from Wells what had happened. When the building was almost finished, cracks appeared in the South Transept and he was forced to suffer the humiliation of seeking the advice of a local firm of builders regarding the underpinning of the foundations. This he did at his own expense, with ever-worsening relations with his client who had no sympathy with his adopted philosophy. In the end Lethaby came close to breakdown and even refused his fee. An excerpt from a letter to his sister-in-law gives a flavour of his anxiety:

> The <u>responsibility</u> of building always withers me up, and now that the cost has mounted up terribly in a scheme of my own to build <u>without</u> a contractor, it is quite terrible to wake to a doubt of the foundations. On going into it a little with my lieutenant I fancy it is entirely my own neglect (as it would be called). [Lethaby's emphasis]

And again, at around the same time, in a letter to a Mr. Cockerell (almost certainly Sydney Cockerell, 1867–1862, later knighted, museum curator and fellow SPAB member):

> I am passing through a time of great anxiety relative to the little church I have been building near here by labour directly hired and no other responsibility than my own, I have muddled and made mistakes on a scheme which only provides for success. Now the foundations seem to me maybe inadequate and for weeks my soul and frame has [sic] been quaking and I am feared of all sorts.[22]

Despite these difficulties, however, it is doubtful whether the church as it stands could possibly have been built in any other way. In accordance with Ruskin's observations in 'The Lamp of Life' (chapter v of *The Seven Lamps of Architecture*), there are many inaccuracies, both subtle and glaring, within the building and which serve to give it a sense of vitality unusual in most buildings of the era. Had regular contractors been hired, such inaccuracies would most likely have had to have been specified. This would hardly have accorded with Ruskin's intentions, for it would once again have removed the freedom of the workman to act out of a sense of ownership and participation. Indeed, Lethaby himself recognises this in his later book *Architecture* (1911)

> ... it was seen that old work was full of variations which seemed to be accidents, and our contract workmen were carefully instructed in jointing, tooling and texture, so that their work might have the same old eager mastery; for still it was thought that if the appearance were reached the essence itself of Gothicness must be present.[23]

The implication being that this approach, which he saw as prevalent in Gothic Revival buildings and crass church 'restorations', was misguided and that only by allowing *authentic* freedom could the true spirit of 'Gothic' be realised.

Variety

Variety, for Ruskin, is the next most important attribute of 'Gothic' after inaccuracy. Where detailing on a building is all of one kind, such as that on a Greek temple, this, he suggested, would signify the enslavement of the workforce. Variety, on the other hand, not only gave evidence of its relative freedom, but also of its concordance with Natural forms.

> we must no more expect to derive either pleasure or profit from an architecture whose ornaments are of one pattern, and whose pillars are of one proportion, than we should out of a universe in which the clouds were all of one shape, and the trees all of one size.[24]

As with other forms of art, architecture, for Ruskin, should seek to say new, interesting and entertaining things rather than the same thing over and again.

Such variety of detailing at Brockhampton, although subtle, is nonetheless, clearly abundant.

Naturalism

'Naturalism was Ruskin's third most important attribute of 'Gothic' and we have already seen how inaccuracy and variety in architecture may be seen to reflect those of Nature. Lethaby's interest in the wider relevance of Nature to architecture resulted in his book, *Architecture, Mysticism and Myth*, later rewritten as *Architecture, Nature and Magic*. In these books, Lethaby argued that symbolism within buildings across widely diverse cultures very often had a universal referent and that this was Nature. All cultures have been aware of the movement of heavenly bodies, for example, and have read their own meanings into these, but the representation of the sky on the ceilings of buildings can be found worldwide. (Indeed, although the OED is uncertain of the origin of the word 'ceiling', it says that there are two spellings, the other being cieling. 'Ciel' is, of course, the French for 'heavens').

Peter Davey, in his book *Arts and Crafts Architecture*, discerns a 'Cosmos-like symbolism'[25] in the church, although does not elaborate.

I suspect from this bare statement that it is a natural assumption based on the fact that Lethaby wrote so much on architectural symbolism. And while it is important to note that, for Lethaby, the search for a symbolism suited to contemporary society was an abiding concern, geometric symbolism within the church is, in reality, far from obvious. For Lethaby's own explanation we might usefully turn to his book *Architecture* (1911) in which he states:

> Proportion, properly, is the resultant of fitness. The Greeks, as their temple architecture slowly developed, came to think that a special virtue attached itself to dimensional simplicity, that, if every part were related to every other part by a simple scheme of fractions, a unity would result, and that the temple in reaching this unity would become a perfect thing. But all such ideas break down where building becomes more complex and is conditioned by other needs than that of obtaining a sort of sacred perfection. Proportion of this sort was in truth rather a satisfaction to the mind than to the eye.[26]

What to look for in Brockhampton Church

The church is situated high above the eastern bank of the River Wye (although this is not apparent whilst visiting), about six miles north of Ross-on-Wye in Herefordshire (grid ref. 594322). Its orientation is precisely to the points of the compass with the main entrance on the southern elevation (Figure 2, overleaf).

Geometric and Other Proportions

In the floor plan drawn from measurements taken in the church, I chose to use imperial units because I assumed that these would have been the units employed during the design and construction, and that any obvious correlations or geometric proportions might better emerge in this way. As will be seen from the drawing, however, neither of these appears to be the case to any notable extent. There are a few exceptions, such as the width of the large stone arches in the nave being 2 feet, and the inner door opening being 4 feet. On the whole, however, the dimensions found in the building seem to bear little correspondence to these units. Any close approximations of geometric proportions appear rather to have been paced-out rather than measured, and even these could be entirely coincidental (for example the bell tower external dimensions being within 9-inches of the crossing tower internal dimensions or the nave length being only 1′ 8″ more than half the total length). A mysterious unit of measurement appears to have been employed here. A clue to what this might have been may be found in the writings of Viollet-le-Duc, who, as has already been noted, appears on Lethaby's 'reading list'. He states that:

> With the mediaeval architects of France the only scale admitted is man; all the points of the building have reference to his stature … and

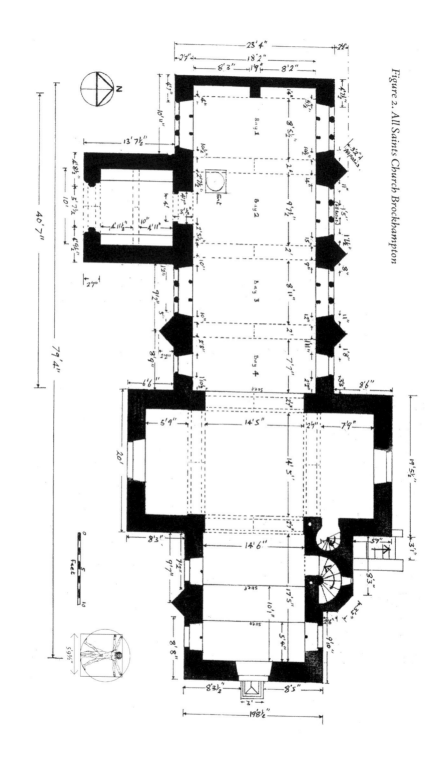

Figure 2. All Saints Church Brockhampton

from this principle necessarily springs the unity of the whole; it has also the advantage of presenting to the eye the real dimensions of the building, since the point of comparison is man himself.[27]

I do not know how tall Lethaby was, nor Randall Wells, but taking the average height of a man to be between about 5'7" and 6' (probably taller today) I looked again at the overall dimensions of the church to judge whether this may have been a basis for measurement. The main entrance into the porch is 5'7½" wide. It is generally acknowledged that the widest arm span between the tips of the fingers equals a person's height. If, then, the overall layout of the church was measured using outstretched arms, we must allow for some inaccuracies; moreover, we must also allow for the possibility that it was not all measured by the same man. The nave length of 40'7" is not exactly divisible by 5'7½". But if we divide it by 7 (a suitably significant number, relating to the number of heavenly bodies known in ancient times, upon which Lethaby devoted an entire chapter of *Architecture, Mysticism & Myth* – Ch. VI), we get the figure 5'9½". This is obviously perfectly concordant with the 'stature of a man'. The nave width is not so neat, being a little over 3 × 5'9½", although the chancel length is within half an inch of 3 × 5'9½" from the eastern crossing arch to the east wall (the number 3, of course, also being significant in this context) and its width, as well as the internal sides of the crossing tower, 2½ times 5'9½". The south transept is also 5'9" deep to within an inch. Perhaps we can conclude from this that Lethaby was, indeed, 5'9½" tall. It would be interesting to find out. It is pertinent to note that Le Corbusier later used a similarly derived scale for the same reasons and called it the 'modular', which was 2260mm, the height of a man with hand stretched upwards.

Using 'the stature of man' as a unit of measurement is itself highly symbolic as is the use of significant (if rather obvious) numerology; for example the four bays in the nave (seasons, evangelists etc.) in addition to the 7 and 3 proportions already mentioned. It is worth returning to Viollet-le-Duc on this matter:

> If, while adopting the principle of the human scale, we employ a system of geometrical proportions, as the architects of antiquity and those of the middle-ages evidently did, we unite two elements of design that compel us to remain true as regards the expression of dimension, and to establish harmonious relations between all the parts.[28]

To this end, Lethaby appears to have used a 'double-cube' for the porch/bell tower, the upper one being slightly smaller than the lower. The roof of this tower is a square-based pyramid formed of four equilateral ('perfect') triangles (giving a theoretical pitch of 54.7°) and the gables of the transepts and chancel are also drawn to be 'perfect' triangles of 60° (in reality 57°). The pitch of the nave roof is 52°. Given Lethaby's design philosophy, it is probably not insignificant that the latitude of the Church is almost exactly 52°N (51.986°N) The crossing tower interior is almost a double-cube although there is evidence that this was altered during construction as will be discussed in due course.

Decorative Symbolism

Decorative symbolism of the sort explored in Lethaby's book *Architecture, Mysticism & Myth* is used sparingly within the church. Among the more prominent examples are the carved stone plaques in the porch above the south door depicting, at the top, an equal cross with four stars below which are plaques depicting doves in flight (Figure 3). Directly below these on the main doors are unusual plaited strap-hinges (these also appear on the eastern vestry door). The plaited hinges (Figure 4) are reminiscent of the entwined serpents which support the Tripod of Plataea at Delphi (Figure 5)

Figure 3. Examples of the carved stone plaques above the south door.

Figure 4. Plaited door hinges.

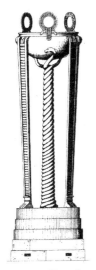

Figure 5. Tripod of Plataea, Delphi

with which Lethaby would have been familiar from his studies of Delphi in *Architecture Mysticism & Myth* (pp.71–3). This is most likely to be a representation of the Biblical reference: 'wise as serpents, harmless as doves' (Matthew 10, v 16).

The choir stalls are constructed in light oak and are decorated with carved depictions of local flora, each plant being itself symbolic. A lengthy document tracing these particular symbolic references was found during archive searches.

The wavy line motif, prominent above the east window and also appearing on the crossing tower waterspout and on the wooden corners of the bell-tower is variously held to represent clouds, or the sea of heaven. It has been employed on the more recent electric light fittings.

The north transept window is arguably the most striking in the building (Figure 6, overleaf). Its unusual design might perhaps be understood from an excerpt from an article Lethaby later wrote for 'The Builder' in 1918:

'The knot of interlacing thread work is also another universal pattern idea suitable for window fillings. All these expedients are ours to use, for they embody universal principles. Theophilus, the twelfth century writer on art speaks of devising the lead glazing of windows in knot patterns, and several such survive at Salisbury and York.'[29]

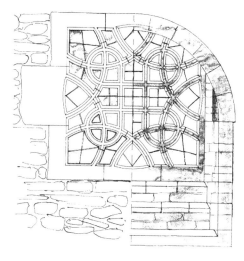

Figure 6. Lethaby's drawing of the south trancept window. Above, the finished window.

Stone

Almost the entire building is of local sandstones. Lethaby states in his specification:

> The stone for walling, footings, and dressings to be obtained from quarries on the estate, to be carefully picked, sound and of even quality. To be worked to lie on its natural bed when set ... [30]

The stone is of two types: grey grit sandstone and red sandstone. These are mixed apparently without any contrived order – as, indeed, they naturally occur locally – both in the rubble walls as well as in window tracery and stone dressings.

On the exterior the stone is left bare, whilst on the interior the rubble walls and roughly dressed stone elements ('axed faced' in Lethaby's specification) are pointed and whitewashed. There is no plaster used in the main body of the church and the ashlar elements, voussoirs, quoins, mouldings etc. which, inside, are predominantly of the red sandstone, are also left bare. These elements have a good, but by no means a high, finish and tooling marks can be easily found, as can prominent masons' marks.

Windows

The windows are all fitted into either mullions (nave and chancel side windows) or into stone tracery with the exception of the six opening lights in the side windows which are fitted into wrought iron frames, themselves fitted into the stone. Pevsner suggested that the South Transept window tracery was formed of concrete[31]. In this he was not correct, it is in fact entirely of cut stone as, indeed, are all the elements of tracery.

The side windows in the nave are unusual for a church, feeling somewhat domestic in scale and design. Each bay in the nave with the exception of that taken by the door, and the last bay before the crossing (marked bay 4 on the drawing, which has smaller windows) is fitted with triple-light mullioned windows. These are set close to the outer face of the wall leaving deep embrasures beneath flat headers, these supported on the inside by detached pillars mirroring the mullions. The width of the embrasures in each of the five openings varies between 7'1½" and 7'3". The more striking, however, is their apparent symmetry within their respective bays, which subsequently proves to be illusory. On the north side, the window opening in bay 1 is offset to the west by 2½", in bay 2 it's only ½", to the west. In bay 3, 1½", to the west and in bay 4, 1½" to the west. On the south wall, the window opening in bay 1 is offset by 3¼" to the west and in bay 3, by 1", again to the west. In bay 4 it is offset by by 2¼" to the east. The most perplexing question in my mind is this: how can an architect specify such inaccuracy? Left to himself, any builder worth the name would have ensured that these window openings were central within their bays. Must the architect insist that no tape measures, sticks or lengths of string are available? Must he insist that men of various statures measure only with their thumbs in order to attain the desired effect? In the case of these windows we might also note that six of the seven windows are offset to the west and one to the east. Are we to read symbolism into this, or is it just chance?

Vaults

Possibly one of the most well-known aspects of this building is that it is roofed by a concrete vault. This was cast over rough boards a bay at a time and supported on the high stone arches (Figure 7). It is not reinforced but, like any traditional vault, uses the principle of compression to remain in place. Although the use of concrete was novel in buildings at this time, a clear precedent had been set 2000 years previously by the Romans who had constructed large mass concrete roofs on buildings such as the Pantheon. Lethaby had an abiding interest in Roman architecture, about which he subsequently wrote a book entitled *Londinium, Architecture and the Crafts* (Duckworth

Figure 7. The concrete vaults under construction.

Figure 8. The Melsetter chapel concrete tunnel vault.

1923). Brockhampton church was his second experiment with mass concrete; the first was a small chapel built at Melsetter on the Orkney Island of Hoy. Here Lethaby had created a concrete 'tunnel vault' (Figure 8). He subsequently submitted a competition design for Liverpool Cathedral which was to have been constructed almost entirely of concrete.

Nave Arches

Among the most striking features of the church are the three steep pointed stone arches in the nave. A likely precedent for this is the 'new' church at Bothenhampton, near Bridport in Dorset, designed by Edward Prior, a close friend of Lethaby who had worked along-side him in Shaw's office and with whom he had collaborated on an earlier church scheme at Symondsbury, Dorset in the early 1880s. Bothenhampton church was begun in 1887 and consecrated in 1890. Given the closeness of the two men and their common ideas and interests, it is certain that Lethaby would have been familiar with Prior's building. Here, then, in Prior's scheme, some 14 years before Lethaby's at Brockhampton, are the three large and imposing stone arches in the nave (Figure 9.). Indeed these are strikingly similar in scale and with a similar chamfered finish. Their springings are also alike, emerging from low in the walls without any corbelling, bases

Figure 9. The stone arches in Bothenhampton nave.

Figures 10 and 11. The arch springings in, left, Bothenhampton and, right, Brockhampton naves.

or plinths (Figures 10 and 11). The original scheme for Brockhampton was for a tiled roof on a timber structure supported on the stone arches (Figure 12), as at Bothenhampton. This was altered, firstly to thatch over concrete vaulted transepts and thatch over a timber structure in the nave and chancel, and later to the complete concrete vault (Figure 13). Note the additional chancel arch, which would have supported timber purlins, but which was not needed for the concrete vault and so omitted during construction).

Prior's arches at Bothenhampton are equally-spaced at 11'5", whereas Lethaby's are not. There seems to be no obvious structural or layout reason why these should not also have been equally spaced between the west wall and the western crossing arch. The attached plan drawn from measurements taken at the church shows the true state of affairs with the dimensions as follows:

West wall to arch no.1 (bay 1): 8'5½"
Arch no.1 to arch no.2 (bay 2): 9'7½"
Arch no.2 to arch no.3 (bay 3): 8'11"
Arch no.3 to crossing arch (bay 4): 7'7"

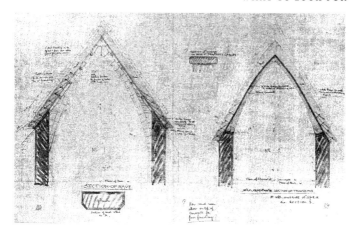

Figure 12. Lethaby's original drawings for the vaults.

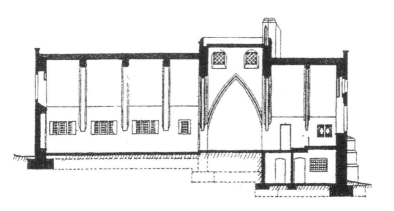

*Figure 13. John Brandon-Jones's copy of Lethaby's original drawing.
Note the extra stone arch in the chancel which was not built*

Figure 14. The south doorway at Bothenhampton

In the case of Brockhampton, beyond the 'fixed scorn' of wilful inaccuracy recommended by Ruskin, it is worth noting that it is the entrance bay (marked 'bay 2' on the drawing) which is the widest, with the other bays becoming progressively narrower as they recede from this. I have been unable to discern any definite pattern or unit of measurement in the spacing of these arches, but, given that they do narrow beyond the entrance bay, it succeeds in giving the illusion that the nave is longer than it actually is. When we enter, we are aware of the vaulted bay in which we find ourselves (bay 2) and naturally assume the others to be of similar dimensions. If this were to have been the case, the nave would be almost 4 feet longer than it is. There may, of course, be more to it than this which I have not unearthed, yet this effect at least (rather than its reverse which would have obtained had bay 2 been the narrowest) seems to have been deliberate.

A further possible borrowing from Prior's church at Bothenhampton is the thickening of the wall between the porch and the nave through which the main south door is pierced, giving the impression of a generally massively thick wall (six feet in the case of Bothenhampton, see Figure 14). At Brockhampton the wall at the south door is 36½" thick and the walls in general are 31", but even this relatively small difference serves to give the impression of an even more substantial building than is actually the case.

Roof

Outside, the roof is thatched in the local tradition, originally using iron fixings in the concrete (now stainless-steel). It has already been noted that the original scheme was for a tiled or slated roof. The coped-gables, unusual on thatched roofs, may be a remnant of this earlier idea.

Thatching was a favourite roofing material for many of the Arts and Crafts architects because it was firstly natural, secondly traditional, and thirdly easily available and cheap (this last point being no longer the case). Its down-side was susceptibility to fire. Many of the Arts and Crafts buildings, originally thatched, suffered serious fires and were subsequently rebuilt using different roofing materials. Examples include: Prior's 'Barn' near Exmouth, Devon; Gimson's 'Stoneywell', near Leicester and Blow's 'Hilles' near Painswick in Gloucestershire. It is by virtue, perhaps, of the concrete understructure of Brockhampton Church that the building has survived unscathed. It remains one of the few Arts and Crafts buildings to retain thatch as a roof covering.

Original Heating

Beneath the floor of the crossing and nave are a series of chambers and a long narrow connecting passage (Figure 15). These are the remnants of the original warm air heating system which was fired by a coke-boiler (the flue, still in use with the current system, runs up inside the wall of the stair-turret). This boiler heated large radiators in the chambers (Figure 16). The heated air in these chambers was then directly convected into the church via four 12" cylindrical clay pipes set within the walls. Fresh cold air would be drawn in from the west end via the low passage and into the chambers. The warm air entered the main body of the church through carved stone grilles

Figure 15. The access and air intake passage in the basement. Note the modern duct above.

Figure 16. One of the radiators, now redundant.

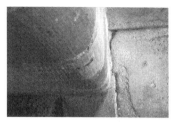

Figure 17. The remaining carved stone grille

Figure 18. The bull-nosed moulding around the south door.

(Figure 17). Only one of these remains (behind the font, and is not now used) as the latest oil-fired blown air system requires its own specialist grilles. The other original ducts remain in use, however, and the position of the outlets is unchanged. As has been mentioned already in relation to the concrete vaults, Lethaby had a great interest in Roman building techniques. It is tempting to suppose that his wall ducts owed their conception to Roman *tubuli i.e.* the clay ducts built into walls in Roman baths etc., and the system in general to an updated version of the hypocaust.

Basement Construction

The construction of the chambers and passage is extremely crude in comparison with the rest of the building, being predominantly of rubble stone and roughly shuttered concrete walls with a concrete ceiling formed over corrugated-iron sheets which remain *in situ*. The whole effect has more of the ambience of Great War trenches about it than of a Herefordshire church.

The floor of the chancel is also a concrete slab, although this is flat on its underside where it forms the ceiling to the vestry. It was specified by Lethaby to be 7" thick and is not reinforced.

Mouldings and Detailing

On the face of it, one would ordinarily suppose that the unity of a building would be aided through similar treatment of detailing throughout. Indeed, this notion is commonplace. It comes of something of a surprise, then, to discover that in Brockhampton Church, which presents nothing if not an impression of unity, barely two details are treated alike. The openings provide the best examples. The inside of the south doorway is a segmental arch with a bullnosed edge from the floor and around the arch (Figure 18). The west window opening inside is fully round headed and bullnosed around the arch and down the reveals, though with a smaller radiused bullnose than that used on the doorway. The nave window openings are flat-headed with detached 'double interlocking' pillars and retain their arrises all round – cills, headers and reveals. The chancel windows are less widely revealed than those in the nave, are narrower and fitted with tracery, but otherwise of similar construction being flat-headed with detached pillars. Here, however, the cills, headers and reveals are all chamfered (Figure 19). The south transept window opening inside is round-headed, like the west window, but here only the arch itself is bullnosed, the reveals retaining their arrises. The north transept window opening is similarly treated but with a stepped and chamfered cill, while the east window has a chamfered triangular header. The door surround to the vestry has a rounded chamfer on the outside all around. The tower windows are of two types: north and south have round-headed, bullnosed arches with rubble arrised reveals, all whitewashed; east and west have triangular-headers on stepped corbels to rubble reveals with arrises and whitewash all around (Figure 20).

Figure 19. Chancel windows.   *Figure 20. Tower windows.*

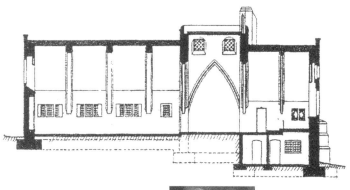

Figure 21. North tower
internal elevation drawing
and photograph.

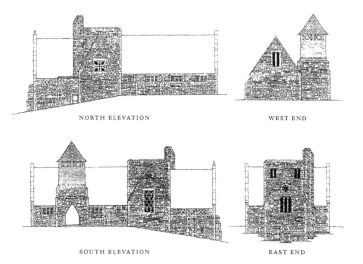

NORTH ELEVATION   WEST END

SOUTH ELEVATION   EAST END

Figure 21. John Brandon-Jones's elevations copied from Lethaby's original
contract drawings

Tower

Pevsner describes the main crossing tower as 'blunt'[32], while Davey says of it that " ... though it has dramatic effect on the interior, [it] is not stressed as it would be in a traditional church.'[33] The available literature asserts that Randall Wells, Lethaby's assistant, raised the crossing tower eight to ten feet in his absence without authorisation.[34] In the literature consulted, however, it is nowhere stated whether Lethaby subsequently insisted that this extra height be removed in order to accord with his original concept, or whether – in line with established Arts and Crafts principles of the need to encourage freedom of expression by those involved in architectural projects – Wells' unauthorised extension was allowed to remain. Lethaby's original contract drawings (Figures 21 and 22) do show a lower tower suggesting that the final form may be Wells's rather than Lethaby's. Alternatively it is possible that the decision to use concrete and thatch rather than the originally planned timber and tiles shown on this drawing necessitated a greater tower height in order to keep the tower windows clear of the thicker roofs and that this decision was Lethaby's. My researches in this regard have, however, proved inconclusive.

Conclusion

My original aim of this study had simply been to come to a better understanding of how the aesthetics of the church work. However, given Lethaby's own extensive writing on the subject of symbolism, it came as something of a surprise during my research to discover that these worked largely according to the principles clearly laid down by Ruskin in 'The Nature of Gothic'. The building itself can thus be seen to have been an architectural experiment to test predominantly Ruskin's hypotheses. Certainly such principles do not necessarily determine the form, proportions or size of this, or any other, building, but they do inform the methods of construction, the working practices and much of the detailing, and it is these more than anything which gives the building its 'flavour'. This, then, has had the effect of shifting the focus to some extent, from Lethaby and onto Ruskin, and to a lesser extent, on the other writers cited. Brockhampton Church, then, allows us to judge whether these theories are thus validated in practice rather than as simply literary ideas. The fact that the church is acclaimed by Pevsner[35] and Jenkins[36] explicitly as successfully expressing the mediaeval without anywhere copying mediaeval forms suggests that Ruskin in particular has, to this extent, been shown to have been correct.

That Lethaby built no more buildings suggests that Ruskin's (and Morris's) ideas about direct labour and other unconventional working practices may have been more problematic. Lethaby had spent much of his working life attempting to ensure that hands-on experience was central to the creation of art and architecture, with a high degree of success. However, simply because his experiments with this on a relatively large scale had brought him close to breakdown, did not necessarily invalidate the principle. Where Lethaby left off, others followed in the same vein with their own varying degrees of success, among them were Randall Wells, Detmar Blow and Ernest Gimson, to name only three[37]. Perhaps we cannot say that Ruskin and Morris, and even Lethaby himself, were wrong in this – indeed, Lethaby never ceased to advocate it in principle – only that it required a more appropriate education (as well as an insurance policy and perhaps a more understanding client) to properly succeed.

It seems to have become accepted wisdom among some commentators that Lethaby's career essentially consisted of three distinct stages: 1) early, classically influenced stage to late 1880s; 2) Arts and Crafts stage (late 1880s to 1911); and 3) Proto-modernist stage concerned with construction technology and a turning-away from earlier aesthetic ideals (1911 to his death in 1931). I have come to doubt this rather neat analysis. Of course there was an evolution in Lethaby's career, as is to be expected. But, certainly from the time he set up his own practice in 1889, and quite probably from before this time, Lethaby was a prolific and tireless advocate for a practically-based approach to good design. In this view he never deviated; thus his emphasis on hand-craft skills rather than on theoretical design; on familiarity with materials and locally relevant building forms rather than the persistent study of historic architectural 'styles'. Lethaby, and the Arts and Crafts movement generally, sought to be directed in their work, not through adherence to some arbitrary style or another, but through addressing practical problems in a pleasing and fitting manner. Beauty, he consistently believed, would inevitably follow where all the relevant criteria had been recognised in a well-executed design and construction. In the harsh light of much subsequent technologically excellent, but aesthetically disastrous building, we might consider this view to have been somewhat naïve – but I'm not sure we'd be justified in this. It might just as easily reflect badly on some of the icons of modernism insofar as they failed to account for such important criteria as, for example, human scale, historical context or wet climates. Above all, Lethaby believed in the evolution of architecture – to be sure, an architecture which could welcome the use of novel materials, but one which would evolve their use from proven traditional forms.

Lethaby maintained his Morrisian socialism throughout his life, advocating meaningful creative work even as industrial pro-duction methods overran architecture and building construction. His emphasis on honesty to materials and the decorative display of structural realities eventually earned him the dubious accolade as a 'pioneer of modernism'. Lethaby dismissed this (as did Voysey) and, somewhat perceptively, said of the Modernist Movement that it was 'only another design humbug to pass off with a shrug – ye olde modernist style …'[38]

The mistake, I suggest, is to see Lethaby's interest in symbolism and aesthetics and later in structural engineering as being necessar-ily separate and incompatible concerns when in fact were all seen by him as integral to architecture and which must all follow from well-conceived and relevant design and construction process-es. Brockhampton Church remains, to this day, a rare testament to the veracity of this belief.

NOTES

1   Pevsner, N. *The Buildings of England; Herefordshire*. Penguin.1963. p.90

2   Jenkins, S. *England's Thousand Best Churches*. Allen Lane;Penguin Press. 1999 p.266

3   Davey, P.*Architects of the Arts and Crafts Movement*. Phaidon. 1995. p. 32

4   Rubens, G. W.R. *Lethaby; His Life and His Work 1857–1931*. The Architectural Press. London.1986. p.206

5   Rubens, G. *W.R.Lethaby; His Life and His Work 1857–1931*. The Architectural Press. London.1986 p.204

6   Rubens, G. *W.R.Lethaby; His Life and His Work 1857–1931*. The Architectural Press. London.1986 p.208

7   Drury, M. *Wandering Architects; in Pursuit of an Arts & Crafts Ideal*. Shaun Tyas. 2000. p.148

8   (Sadly these appear to have 'gone missing' from the RIBA archive. Copies of copies of as many as I have been able to find are reproduced throughout this study).

9   Rubens, G. *W.R.Lethaby; His Life and His Work 1857–1931*. The Architectural Press. London.1986 p. 206/7

10 Pevsner, N. *The Buildings of England; Herefordshire*. Penguin.1963 p.90

11 Cf. MacCarthy, F. *William Morris* Faber and Faber. London.1994 p.617

12 Rubens, G. *W.R.Lethaby; His Life and His Work 1857–1931*. The Architectural Press. London.1986 p.74

13 Rubens, G. *W.R.Lethaby; His Life and His Work 1857–1931*. The Architectural Press. London.1986 p.75

14 Cf. John Ruskin. 'The Nature of Gothic' in *The Stones of Venice (Vol II)*. John Wiley & Sons. N.Y. 1886 p.159

15 Ibid.

16 Ibid. p.160

17 Ibid. p.163

18   J. Ruskin. *The Seven Lamps of Architecture.* George Allen.1894 p.303

19   Ibid. p.170

20   Ibid. p.230

21   Ibid. (pp. 169-170)

22   Ibid.

23   W.R.Lethaby. *Architecture* Williams & Norgate 1911. p.238

24   J. Ruskin.'The Nature of Gothic' in *The Stones of Venice (Vol.II)* John Wiley & Sons. NY.1886. p.175

25   Davey, P. *Arts and Crafts Architecture.* Phaidon. London 1995 p.69

26   W.R.Lethaby. *Architecture* Williams & Norgate 1911. p. 240

27   Viollet-le-Duc, E.E. *The Architectural Theory of Viollet-le-Duc.* M.F.Hearn(ed.) Massachusetts Inst. Of Technology.1990 p.230

28   Ibid. p.230

29   'The Builder' 15/11/1918 p.319

30   Lethaby's specification, p.4

31   Cf. Pevsner, N. *The Buildings of England; Herefordshire.* Penguin.1963 p.90

32   Pevsner, N. *The Buildings of England; Herefordshire.* Penguin.1963 p.90

33   Davey, P. *Arts and Crafts Architecture.* Phaidon. London 1995 p.69

34   Cf. Rubens, G.W.R.*Lethaby; His Life and His Work 1857–1931.* The Architectural Press. London.1986 p.159; Drury, M. *Wandering Architects; in Pursuit of an Arts & Crafts Ideal.* Shaun Tyas. 2000 p.150;

35   Cf. Pevsner, *The Buildings of England* p.90,

36   Cf. Jenkins, S. England's Thousand Best Churches. Allen Lane;Penguin Press. 1999. pp.266–7

37   Cf. Drury, M. *Wandering Architects; in Pursuit of an Arts & Crafts Ideal.* Shaun Tyas. 2000

38   Davey, P. *Arts and Crafts Architecture.* Phaidon. London 1995. p.77

BIBLIOGRAPHY

Backemeyer & Gronberg(eds.) *W.R.Lethaby 1857–1931; Architecture, Design and Education.* Lund Humphries. London 1984

Davey, P. *Arts and Crafts Architecture.* Phaidon. London 1995

Drury, M. *Wandering Architects; in Pursuit of an Arts & Crafts Ideal.* Shaun Tyas. 2000

Garrigan, K.O. *Ruskin on Architecture.* Uni. Of Wisconsin Press.1973

Hilton, T. *John Ruskin; The Later Years* Yale Uni. Press 2000

Jenkins, S. *England's Thousand Best Churches. Allen Lane;Penguin Press. 1999*

Lethaby, W.R. *Architecture, Mysticism and Myth* Solos Press 1994 (1st pub. 1891)

 Architecture, Nature & Magic Duckworth 1956

 Architecture Williams & Norgate 1911

 Londinium, Architecture & the Crafts. Duckworth. 1923

 Letters (Not thought to have been published in full. See appendix iii.)

 Materials specification (Unpublished)

 'A National Architecture' The Builder 15th November 1918 pp.319/20

Mason, H. *All Saints' Church, Brockhampton, Herefordshire* (Illustrated Guide)

MacCarthy, F. *William Morris* Faber and Faber. London.1994

Morris, W. *Morris on Architecture* C. Miele(ed.)Sheffield Academic Press. 1996

Muthesius, H. *The English House* Trans: J. Seligman. Crosby, Lockwood, Staples. London 1979

Pevsner, N. *The Buildings of England; Herefordshire.* Penguin.1963

Pugin, A.W. *The True Principles of Pointed or Christian Architecture. Academy Editions. 1973* (1st pub 1841)

Richardson, M. *Architects of the Arts and Crafts Movement (RIBA Drawings Series)* Trefoil Books Ltd. London 1983

Rubens, G. *W.R.Lethaby; His Life and His Work 1857-1931.* The Architectural Press. London.1986

Ruskin, J. 'The Nature of Gothic' in *The Stones of Venice* John Wiley & Sons. N.Y.1886

 The Seven Lamps of Architecture. George Allen.1894

Viollet-le-Duc, E.E. *The Architectural Theory of Viollet-le-Duc*. M.F.Hearn(ed.)
    Massachusetts Inst. Of Technology.1990
Voysey, C.F.A. *Individuality* Nadder Books.1986 (1st pub. 1915)

ACKNOWLEDGEMENTS

Thanks to Hugo Mason of Hook Mason Architects, Castle Street, Hereford for access to archive material. Thanks also to Patrick Goode and Martin Valatin for their invaluable suggestions and references.

ABOUT THE AUTHOR

Graham Burgess is a graduate in both Philosophy and in Architecture and has run his own architectural practice since 2001.

A private study of Ruskin, Morris, Voysey, Baillie-Scott, Lethaby and others has convinced him of the continuing relevance of an Arts and Crafts philosophy in our own time. He has attempted to follow in the footsteps of some of these earlier pioneers, experimenting with unconventional working practices and more responsive design processes. In doing so, he has succeeded in replicating some of the beauty and vitality of their buildings – as well as some of their difficulties and anxieties. Most of his built work can be found in and around Frome in Somerset.

Graham is also the author of a number of books including *The Nature of Green Building* (2014).

Printed in Great Britain
by Amazon